A STATEMENT OF FACTS

CONCERNING THE

BLOODY RIOT IN WILMINGTON, N. C.

Of Interest to Every Citizen of the United States.

BY REV. J. ALLEN KIRK, D. D.,

Pastor of the Central Baptist Church of Wilmington, N. C.

Bloody Riot Perpetrated upon the Helpless and Inoffensive Negro.

Wilmington, N. C., Thursday, November 10, 1898.

It was clamored among the political campaigners that in the eastern portion of North Carolina, the white people were under Negro rule. They took advantage of this scarecrow, and held it up before the white friends of the Negro in all their political speeches, using also the Manly article to create anger among the loyal and conservative white citizens. It is not my motive to give the nature of the Manly article or the number of Negro officeholders, but to state the facts touching the riot above named. It is my feeling to impartially state to white and colored the facts as I best know them pertaining to the bloody riot.

Ministers Called to Explain.

After the publication of the Manly article, and the threats heaped upon him on the account of its publication, and the withdrawal of its advertisements by its white contributors, and the appeal to the Interdenominational Ministerial Union to help the enterprise, as it would be com-

pelled to die unless the colored people would subscribe
and pay their subscriptions more readily than they had in
the past, Being the only daily paper in the South and
enterprise of its kind, the Ministerial Union promised to
ask their people to subscribe to the paper and support it
as an enterprise of our race, without any thoughts of endorsing the much talked of article, and with this view,
they published the resolution asking the colored people
to support the Record. The ministers being asked to ex-
plain their resolution, drew up a resolution of explanation
and presented it to the Messenger, a white paper, in answer to their request, but it seemed not to be satisfactory,
and they were therefore publicly assailed by the journals
of Wilmington to their sad regret and misfortune; but
we believe that all these steps were taken in order to fur-
ther political ends. There was a meeting called on Wednesday night, November 9th, and the Ministers and leading colored citizens were requested to attend and they
attended; this meeting was white. They were asked to
see to it that Manly leave the City, the colored ministers
stated that they were not concerned in Manly's article, and
had never been. The following extract is taken from the
Wilmington Messenger, white, referring to

The Ministerial Union, Colored.

"Don't forget its members. The Record will be dis-
posed of and its editor relegated to non-residence. So let
it be with the smart elect preachers, who composed the
Union, and endorsed the Record. Let them consider the
propriety of finding more congenial fields upon which to
pasture. They must quit. It might as well be under-
stood now as hereafter. Resignations and non-residence
will be enforced."

There was a request made on the part of the editor of
the Wilmington daily Messenger to all of the white ministers of the various denominations of Wilmington, to
preach from a certain text on a certain Sabbath before
the election and the dire bloody riot, which seemed to
agitate and move the people to reek out their sentiments

coming from the bosom of the editor and not the text in its jistical connection with the scriptures, and with the will of God. The texts were as follows: Isaiah, 17th chapter, 14th verse—"And behold at evening tide trouble; before the morning he is not. This is the portion of them that spoil us, and the lot of them that rob us." It seems that this text is applicable to the Negroes in profession, and the common people, and whereas the Negoes were not robbing them of their material goods, the text points rather to their political interest. The text pertaining to the ministers and their flocks:—Jeremiah, 25th chapter, 35th verse:—"And the shepherds shall have no way to flee, nor the principal of the flock to escape." The white ministers of Wilmington, N. C. carried their guns in the bloody riot.

Election Day.

Tuesday, November 8th, 1898. Perfect peace seemed to pervade but when the sleeping lion should awake and bound upon his prey. All the peaceful Negroes and white people made glad by the following circular:

To the Voters of New Hanover County.

Rev. Dr. Peyton H. Hoge, in a letter to the Governor, of Saturday, November 5th, uses the following language:

"I have seen several prominent members of the campaign committee and have the positive assurances from them that not only is no intimidation contemplated, but that it will be discountenanced by every means in their power."

"If Negroes do as Henderson advised them: go to the polls and cast their ballots quietly and go home; I have no idea that there will be any disturbance."

"I think all the members of our committee feel that their honor is involved in seeing that the agreement is carried out in good faith; and we will certainly use all efforts to secure that result, and we have the same promise from prominent members of the campaign committee."

Dr. Hoge was one of the committee who conferred with

the Governor and agreed upon the compromise which was cordially and almost unanimously approved and ratified by the merchants and business men of the city, and by the Democratic campaign committee.

The Governor has other assurances of similar import from all of the committee that conferred with him. As men of honor they could not do otherwise.

A. E. HOLTON,

Chairman Republican State Ex. Com.

CYRUS THOMPSON,

Chairman People's Party State Ex. Com.

The following circular was issued in consequence of an agreement effected by Governor Russell and the leading Democratic politicians of Wilmington, leading citizens and business men: (The agreement) to put in no county ticket in the field; no Negro nominees, but to have only the State, Congressional and Senatorial tickets.

"Senator Pritchard, Senator Butler, Governor Russell, Chairman Holton and Chairman Thompson and Oliver H. Dockery appeal to the Republicans and Populists of New Hanover County to turn out and vote the State, Congressional and Senatorial tickets.

Conditions are such in your county that we join in giving you this advice. Listen to us! Do not encourage any attempt to depart from the agreement made with the merchants and business men. They have taken down their Legislative Ticket for the House, and have put up their two Representatives. Let us make no objections to them or to their County Ticket. These merchants and business men have given their word that there shall be a free and fair and peaceful election. Now it is most important to you that you turn out and vote the Fusion Ticket for Judges and Solicitor, for Congressman and for State Senator. Do not listen to men who seek to divide you because they themselves have personal grievances or disappointments. Let every Republican, every Populist, every Independent, every man who is opposed to the Democratic Machine and its methods, turn out and put in his vote. If you fail to do it, the consequence may be disastrous.

Vote for the Fusion Ticket, for Oliver H. Dockery for Congress, and R. B. Davis for Senate.

Do not hang around the polls on Election Day, vote and go to your homes.

J. C. PRITCHARD,
MARION BUTLER,
D. L. RUSSELL.

A. E. HOLTON,
Chairman Republican State Committee.
CYRUS THOMPSON,
Chairman Populist State Committee.
OLIVER H. DOCKERY,
Candidate for Congress.

The Negroes were absolutely obedient to the above request; seeing the mighty power that hung over their homes, and carried this order out to the letter, consequently all was peace on the Tuesday of the election. Why should it not be; when they were completely left out of the nomination and the county ticket relegated. In the midst of all this, preparations among our supposed white friends were being made to strike the fearful blow upon the Negroes and on that night, if anything would be started, I did not see it, but heard it from an eye witness, that there was an army of white citizens mobilized in the old field back of Tenth street, on Tuesday night, waiting for signals from the sentinels. (Appointed by the citizens.) They walked their beats through the City all night, but nothing happened on Tuesday night, only a little trouble in the precincts as to ballot boxes. Pistols held in the faces of Negro poll holders who had to leave to save their lives, for the light was extinguished and they knew not what moment they would be killed. This is from the Deputy Sheriff of the County to me, he said the poll holders told him.

Citizens' Mass Meeting, Wednesday, November 9, 1898.

The Evening Dispatch of Wilmington, North Carolina, says: Negro editor Manly must leave the State.

Citizen's Mass Meeting give him twenty-four hours to

get out of the limits—Mayor Wright and Chief Melton must resign.

The mass meeting of citizens and taxpayers called for 11 o'clock met promptly at that hour. There were nearly 2,000 of Wilmington's leading citizens and most prominent business men present and from the determined look on the face of every man no one could doubt the import of the assemblage. On motion, Col. A. M. Waddell was called to the Chair and after mounting the rostrum called the meeting to order. The court room was packed to suffocation, but as the chairman arose to address the meeting, the drop of a pin could have been heard.

Col. Waddell stated that the first business of the meeting was the consideration of a resolution which he had to read to them.

Col. Waddell then read the resolution which space prevent our publishing in full. The preamble declared that this community would no longer be ruled by men of African origin; that our eyes are open to the fact that we must act now or leave our children to a gloomy fate; that we propose in the future to give employment as far as possible only to white men.

Then followed the paragraph relating to the Manly article which we give in full, as follows:

"That we have been, in our desire for harmony and peace, blinded both to our best interests and rights. A climax was reached when the Negro paper of this city published an article so vile and slanderous that it would in most communities have resulted in the lynching of the editor. We deprecate lynching and yet there is no punishment provided by the courts adequate for the offense. We therefore owe it to the people of this community and this city, as a protection against such license in the future, that the paper known as the Record cease to be published and that its editor be banished from this community.

"We demand that he leave this city within twenty-four hours after the issuance of this proclamation. Second, that the printing press from which the 'Record' has been issued be packed and shipped from the city without delay, that we be notified within twelve hours of the acceptance or rejection of this demand.

"If the demand is agreed to, within twelve hours, we counsel forbearance on the part of all white men. If the demand is refused or if no answer is given within the time mentioned then the editor, Manly, will be expelled by force."

Several amendments were offered and rejected as being against law and order. On motion, a committee of five, consisting of Colonel Walker Taylor and Messrs. George Roundtree, S. H. Fishblate, Iredell Meares and Hugh McRae, was appointed to consider the resolution and report to the meeting. During the absence of the committee loud calls were made for Colonel Waddell, and he responded briefly, heartily endorsing the resolution. As he concluded cheers were made for our new Congressman, Hon. John D. Bellamy, and he too, responded with a rousing speech. Others that spoke were Frank McNeil, Esq., Judge Borneman, Junius Davis, Esq., and P. B. Manning, Esq.

At this juncture the committee returned and reported that it endorsed the resolutions heartily and they were then adopted by the meeting and every man present affixed his signature.

The committee also reported the following resolution, which was unanimously adopted with rousing cheers:

"Resolved, We, the undersigned citizens in mass meeting assembled do agree that Mayor S. P. Wright and Chief of Police John R. Melton have shown their inability to give this city a decent government and their administration has not provided protection for our citizens, but has rather proven a menace to this community and they ought to resign.

"On motion, the chair appointed a committee of twenty-five citizens to carry out the action of the meeting and also carry into operation such other plans as may come up, such as selecting a new Board of Aldermen, etc. After adopting resolutions of minor importance, thanking the city and foreign press and various committees, the first meeting of its kind ever held in North Carolina, adjourned.

"Manly must leave by to-morrow, noon, and Wright and Melton must resign."

A member of this meeting arose and asked the question
of the Chairman: "What shall we do with the ministers?"
We know not what the answer was, but we know the
action, for we are exiled and scattered over the country
from our pulpits and our people, without having time to
get our property or our money or any other means of
protection for our families, but left them in the woods
and country places to flee for our lives, hoping that we
might be able to gather them home at some future time
and in a place of safety. Special reference to the Boston
Negro was published in the Evening Dispatch. It was
supposed to have been directed to J. Allen Kirk, pastor
of the Central Baptist Church, of Wilmington, North
Carolina. The reference reads as follows: "The Negro
who came from Boston here to lead the Negroes in their
depredations had better take his departure and shake the
dust of the city from his feet."

But this divine has never taken any part in politics and
plead continually that his people follow peace and order
and even was a member of the committee (the Chairman)
that drew up a resolution of prayer and fasting on the
part of his people to go into effect Monday, November
7th, prior to the election, and the much regretted riot.
Notwithstanding that, he had ofttimes invoked the blessings
of God upon the City of Wilmington, upon white and
colored and all enterprises carried on by them. It seems
that the inevitable came. O! The poor helpless Negro.
God help him, and may all that read the following and
impartial story, white and black, pray that God may stay
the strong arm of our white brethren and all our colored
brethren from shedding blood. My heart is burdened
with the cares of our race; and with anxiety I appeal and
entreat our white brethren to help us to quell the many
disturbances that are now happening in our country. With
impartiality, love and respect toward white and colored
I give the following statements of the Wilmington Riot
as best known to me. Not with the intention of moving
the passions of white or colored men, but that I may prevent exaggerated stories from being heaped upon the community or upon the country.

Wednesday there was a great Jubilee march by the Democrats through the City, probably five hundred in number, and report after report could be heard from their guns. The cheers and loud hurrahs and shrieks in the streets were enough to intimidate and demoralize all peaceful citizens and to send fear and terror to the hearts of the Negroes inhabiting the City of Wilmington. But it cleared away and we thought all was over and Dr. Kirk being at Major Walker's, whose wife receiving a telephone that the whites were gathering around Castle Street in great numbers with guns and arms of various kinds and advised her not to sleep that night, but to keep her eyes open. The Rev. started home to see about his family and as he got to Fanning Street the firing began; not knowing the nature of it he sends for his family and he and his family lodged in the suburbs of the City that night. Returning home the next morning he arose from the breakfast table and went to see what the signs of the times were. He saw a young man rushing by on his wheel whom he called to and asked what the trouble was, he said they were all gathering at the Armory on Market Street, preparing to burn the Record. Rev. Kirk started for a carriage to remove his family but they were then coming and he took his family to the suburbs of the City, hiding in the Colored Cemetery until the disturbances of the day were quite over; having messengers to go back and forth to bring him the news of all that was done. This he kept up until the chief fighting was over. They marched down to the Love and Charity Hall, went in, threw out the press into the street and the building burned down. Then they marched to Rev. J. Allen Kirk's house, pastor of the Central Baptist Church, and the Regulators lined up in front of the parsonage, while two came to the door and knocked for entrance, but they were told that he and his family had gone. They went from there across the railroad into what is known as Darktown and Brooklyn; they had sent a committee to remove all the white women and their children down town, where they had prepared a guard to keep them secure. They marched through the streets protected by these military and citizen regulators, perfectly safe.

It was a great sight to see them marching from death, and
the colored women, colored men, colored children, colored
enterprises and colored people all exposed to death. Firing began, and it seemed like a mighty battle in war time.
The shrieks and screams of children, of mothers, of wives
were heard, such as caused the blood of the most inhuman
person to creep. Thousands of women, children and men
rushed to the swamps and there lay upon the earth in the
cold to freeze and starve. The woods were filled with
colored people. The streets were dotted with their dead
bodies. A white gentleman said that he saw ten bodies
lying in the undertakers office at one time. Some of their
bodies were left lying in the streets until up in the next
day following the riot. Some were found by the stench
and miasma that came forth from their decaying bodies
under their houses. Every colored man who passed
through the streets had either to be guarded by one of
the crowd or have a paper (pass) giving him the right to
pass. All colored men at the cotton press and oil mills
were ordered not to leave their labor but stop there, while
their wives and children were shrieking and crying in the
midst of the flying balls and in sight of the cannons and
Gatling gun. All the white people had gone out of that
part of the City, this army of men marched through the
streets, sword buckled to their sides, giving the command
to fire. Men stood at their labor wringing their hands and
weeping, but they dare not move to the protection of their
homes. And then when they passed through the streets
had to hold up their hands and be searched. The little
white boys of the city searched them and took from them
every means of defence, and if they resisted, they were
shot down. From an eye-witness and a reliable colored
lady, from New York, it was stated that they went into
a colored man's house, he sitting at the fire, they thought
he fired a shot; he ran, they shot him down, then took up
a stick of wood and bursted his brains out; then they went
on firing, it seems, at every living Negro, killing a great
many of them; searching everyone they could get hold
of; this went on all day and night, more or less. The city
was under military rule; no Negro was allowed to come

into the city without being examined or without passing
through with his boss, for whom he labored. Colored
women were examined and their hats taken off and search
was made even under their clothing. They went from
house to house looking for Negroes that they considered
offensive; took arms they had hidden and killed them for
the least expression of manhood. They gathered around
colored homes, firing like great sportsmen firing at rabbits
in an open field and when one would jump his man, from
sixty to one hundred shots would be turned loose upon him.
His escape was impossible. One fellow was walking along
a railroad and they shot him down without any provoca-
tion. It is said by an eye witness that men lay upon
the street dead and dying, while members of their race
walked by helpless and unable to do them any good or
their families. Negro stores were closed and the owners
thereof driven out of the city and even shipped away at
the point of the gun.

Some of the churches were searched for ammunition, and
cannons turned toward the door in the attitude of blowing
up the church if the pastor or officers did not open them
that they might go through. Sunday, November 13th,
while the funeral of a licensed minister was going on in
Central Baptist Church, of which Dr. J. Allen Kirk is
pastor, they, thinking the pastor was preaching, sur-
rounded the church it is supposed in order to capture him
when he came out. Saturday, previous to this, they went
around to the colored ministers and asked them what they
intended to preach on Sunday.

This riot not only touched the Negro, but it touched
the Republican party, for it compelled the Republican
Mayor, Chief of Police, their Aldermen, their policemen,
and all to resign their offices and be sent away from the
city; that is to say, the Mayor and other prominent white
leaders. It is supposed that John C. Dancy is in danger
in Wilmington, N. C.

White ministers carried their guns to kill Negro Chris-
tians and sinners. The mob took the leading colored ministers and compelled them to go around the city with them
and ask the colored people to be obedient to the white

people and go in their homes and keep quiet. This was a great humiliation for us and a shame upon our denominations; and after all this some of them were compelled to leave the city.

Dr. J. Allen Kirk's Escape.

When he left the city with his wife and little Mabel Stitt following him in tears, there was a fusillade of balls flying abroad in the city; he caught up a delivery wagon, put his family in it and insisted that he drive them to the country, which he did, and they went in hiding in the swamps below the Colored Cemetery.

Mrs. J. Allen Kirk a Heroine.

As Mrs. Kirk stood in the Colored graveyard of Wilmington, N. C., with her little niece Mabel, daughter of the deceased pastor of Zion Wesley Church of Philadelphia, Penna., by her side, and her husband before her, the guns roaring around her, like in a mighty battle, she saw that her husband would not leave her, and said to him, "Mr. Kirk, escape for your life, you cannot carry me with you, perhaps they won't kill me, if they do I will die; you go! Go! Mr. Kirk." She is a great and loving wife.

Dr. J. Allen Kirk was determined not to get out of reach of the riot, until he could get the whole story, consequently he had friends who went back and forth and brought him the news of the disturbances in the city. Learning that they had compelled Manly to leave the city, he got on a boat, and in the midst of the tears of his wife and niece and farewell kisses, he sailed down the creek and got off and waded the swamp and went through the wood and by-paths, nine miles from the city. And still he had the news brought to him, even until he took his leave, Sunday evening, November 13th, from Castle Haynes, nine miles from Wilmington. Before leaving home, he called the family with whom he and his wife and little niece were stopping, around the family altar and placed them and himself in the hands of God for protection. He bought his ticket for Weldon, N. C., with the intention of going much farther. When he boarded the train he entered the smoker, and there found that Regulators were on board the train and spotted him at once. They began to curse with refernce to him and to make great threats. He determined to try them to see if they would do him bodily harm. When the train stopped at a couple of stations ahead, he got up, apparently to go out; as soon as he arose they followed to be sure that he did not get out of their sight; he passed into the first class car and they watched him through the glass door. About this time the train was ready to stop at another station, and Lawyer Moore, colored, of Wilmington, N. C., stepped on board the train; seeing Dr. Kirk, and he seeing him, could tell by each other's expression that serious danger and trouble were aboard the train, we, therefore, refrained speaking to each other, or acknowledging that we knew each other. When he boarded the train, they spotted him, and considered that they had two that they would manage to suit their own ideas that night. Lawyer Moore was to get off at Wilson, N. C., and in fact he did get off but was compelled to return to the car. This completely unstrung the most pitiful colored lawyer, for he had heard their threats, their determination to remove him from the earth, or to prevent him from bothering them again. In some way or other, when he came back into the car, Dr. Kirk said he knew why he had come back, to appear ignorant of the cause, and to draw out the Regulators, that sat gazing upon both of us like a lion watching his prey. He asked Lawyer Moore if he was not to stop at Wilson. He said, "yes;" then he asked him where he was going now. He said that he did not know and that he had no money to go anywhere, but he thought he would go as far as Rocky Mount if the conductor would let him. Dr. Kirk said, in order to draw out the Regulators and see what they meant to do, perhaps some of these white gentlemen will give you the money to go as far as Rocky Mount. Then they began to curse and swear and said they would rather send him down to hell, calling him all manner of names, than to

give him his fare to Rocky Mount. When the train blew
for the station, the Regulators passed into the first class
car to consult; the porter passed out of the door and left
it ajar. Lawyer Moore leaped from the car and dashed
through the wood, while the train was in motion, thereby
escaping; but the train was stopped and they went out
to look for him, but he had gone. Then they got back
in the car; we had but a short distance to go before we
reached Rocky Mount. And they began to watch Dr.
Kirk very closely, with what intention the Dr. could not
tell, but he thought and felt that it was as serious as
death. Before the train stopped, it seems that the conductor must have told them that his ticket was for Weldon, and that he would have to be there awhile and it
was not necessary to disturb him on the train. This is
conjecture. Dr. Kirk became very uneasy and prepared
to go out; he got a lunch, hired a carriage and rode all
that night through the storm and reached Whitaker, N.
C. next morning and boarded a freight and came on to
Petersburg, Va.; he promised his wife before he left that
he would send her a telegram (which was a sign) that
next morning from Richmond, Va., if he got there, and
if she received no telegram it was a sign that he was dead.
He could not reach Richmond, he therefore wrote a mes-
sage and gave it to a colored gentleman at Whitaker, N.
C., insisting upon him to be sure and send it, not stating
that he was in North Carolina. This shows the complete
organic strength of this most regretful and dreadful move-
ment going on in North Carolina. The telegraph, the
telephone, and even it seems the very railroad train knows
how to move against the Negro in this matter and the
exiled ones, either colored or white, for both were shipped
from Wilmington and were kept going out of the state.
It is as hard to get out of the State as it was to pass the
ruffians at three Eastern Gates, as you travel through the
East. We are widows' sons. Lord, God, is there no
help for us. Dr. Kirk left his wife in a country hut in
the swamps of North Carolina, sleeping on a pallet waiting to hear from him; and he, a minister of the gospel,
honored and respected by black and white throughout the
country as far as is known to himself and others.

He appeals in the name of humanity that the lives of the citizens of these United States be protected, let them be white or black; for we all fight and die for the same country and her flag. Extend to us the hand of help! Give us the strong grip of the lion! Lift this dark and oppressed race from a dead level of sore affliction to a living perpendicular of consideration in the eyes of this nation. Not from a political standpoint, but an humane, recognizing us as worthy your protection if nothing more.

The above is a limited sketch of the troubles in Wilmington, N. C. The entreaty is to move the feeling of those who may read them. It is not to stir up passion, but pity. It is not to make enemies, but friends. It is not from the heart of an evil thinker, but one that prayeth that God may revolutionize the fearful sentiment of the South, and inspire sympathy and pity in the hearts of our white friends, for good to our race. The summary of the situation: The Evening Dispatch, of Wilmington, N. C., published Friday evening, November 11, 1898, states that a correct list of the fatalities will never be published, but there were many men wounded as well as killed; Negroes and some whites. Says the Dispatch, in the same issue, "A detailed account of the trouble yesterday will never be given—that is a correct statement—as it was impossible in the excitement to get at the details or to recollect them; and the number of Negroes killed and wounded will brobably never be known." An eye witness says that she believes there were more than one hundred destroyed in the said conflict. Dr. Kirk entreats the Negro race to refrain from threats and highhanded talking, and loud and boisterous conduct in the streets. Be considerate in all they do. Conduct themselves as gentlemen and ladies, and try by all means to keep the peace that is necessary to our existence in this country. Ever trusting God, with all their hearts, leaning not unto their own understanding, but in all their ways acknowledging God and He will direct our paths. Amen.

It is generally supposed by the better white citizens, that the Negroes who suffer at the hands of these atrocious mobs, are of the lower or vicious class of our race, but in the case of Wilmington, N. C., the reverse is the truth. For the colored citizens of Wilmington were progressive and enterprising and were characterized by their endeavor to live as worthy citizens. They are property holders, averaging from five to forty thousand dollars, respectively. From their ranks were furnished teachers, lawyers, physicians, clergymen, merchants and business men. The intellectuality of the colored citizens is beyond the average, in so much that it has been recognized by the conservative white people of the city and State. The pastors of the colored churches were recognized by white and colored as the most able divines that ever stood in the pulpits of Wilmington. The membership of the various denominations loved and respected their pastors, because of their ability to lead them in truth and right. There was a great lamentation heard throughout the city when the mob got hold of some of the leading pastors and took them from their members. Their shrieks could be heard across the city in exclamations like these: O! O! My God! My God! Where have they taken our pastor!—from men and women.

The white people of Wilmington intended to remove all the able leaders of the colored race, stating that to do so would leave them better and obedient servants among the Negroes; and all the better class of the colored citizens were driven from the city, showing to the world that they were not after the criminal and ignorant class of Negroes, but the professional and business men. The whites claim that Dr. I. S. Lee, D. D., Rev. Dr. J. Allen Kirk, and lawyer W. E. Henderson were the strongest forces at the head of their race in the city. These and many others with them were driven and sent away from the city.

This postscript is to show to the white and colored people of these United States and the world, that the decent families of our race have been assailed and routed like beasts from their God given positions as leaders of their race.

CPSIA information can be obtained
at www.ICGtesting.com
Printed in the USA
LVHW020803161121
703456LV00003B/113

9 781014 049759